THE
RESPIRATORY SYSTEM:

How Living Creatures Breathe

by
Dr. Alvin Silverstein
and
Virginia B. Silverstein

Illustrated by George Bakacs

Prentice-Hall, Inc.
Englewood Cliffs, N. J.

For Carrie Lee Silverstein

10   9   8   7

THE RESPIRATORY SYSTEM:
HOW LIVING CREATURES BREATHE

© 1969 by *Dr. Alvin Silverstein and Virginia B. Silverstein*

Illustrations © 1969 by Prentice-Hall, Inc.

Library of Congress Catalog Card Number: 68-28376

Printed in the United States of America   •   *J*

Prentice-Hall International, Inc., London
Prentice-Hall of Australia, Pty. Ltd., Sydney
Prentice-Hall of Canada, Ltd., Toronto
Prentice-Hall of India Private Ltd., New Delhi
Prentice-Hall of Japan, Inc., Tokyo

CONTENTS

Also by the authors:

I

Respiration in the Living World

If you hold your hand in front of your nose and mouth as you breathe, you will feel puffs of warm air coming out. This is air that you have just breathed out of your lungs. Between each of these puffs you breathe in again and fill your lungs with new air.

We all breathe in and out thousands of times a day, from the moment we are born to the moment that we die. We do not have to think about breathing. We breathe in and out when we are asleep, just as we do when we are awake.

Although we rarely think about breathing, it is one of the most important functions of our bodies.

It brings in air, which contains the gas we call oxygen. Our bodies, just like the bodies of almost all living creatures, need oxygen to "burn" their fuel. Without the energy that they get from this "burning," they would quickly die.

All the creatures of the earth, from the mightiest whales to the tiniest insects, from the tallest trees to the smallest plants, are made up of tiny living building blocks called cells. Each cell is like a bustling chemical factory. Thousands of different events are going on in each cell of every living thing all the time.

In order for all this activity to take place, the cells need energy. Living organisms get energy by burning food materials. To burn their food, plants and animals need oxygen, a gas which they take in from the air or water, depending on where they live. The manner in which plants and animals take in this oxygen is part of an important process which scientists call respiration.

Different kinds of organisms have different ways of getting oxygen to the cells of their bodies. Many animals have respiratory systems very much like the kind we have. But other animals, such as fish and insects, have systems very different from ours. And the respiratory system in plants is more different still. We shall learn more about these varied systems in the following pages.

2

Our Body

Our respiratory system does not work alone. Its work is closely linked with other systems of the body.

Our bodies are like cities. They are made up of more than 100 trillion different kinds of cells, which work together for the good of the whole organism. Each "factory-cell" takes in endless streams of materials, delivered to it along a system of highways provided by the bloodstream. Some of the materials come in from outside the city (outside the body), while others are sent from one factory (cell) to another.

In cities there are systems, such as communications and transportation systems, which work to help keep the city running smoothly. In the body, too, there are systems, each with special tasks to help keep the organism running smoothly.

The brain and spinal cord and the network of nerves spread through all parts of the body form a communications system, along which information and commands can be sent. Waste materials are sent out of the body by a special garbage collecting and disposal system, which is called the excretory system.

Just as the buildings of the city have frameworks of beams and girders, the body has a framework of bones called the skeleton, which helps to hold it up. The system of muscles also helps to support the body, and helps it to move as well. (Cities do not move, but people do, and our bodies have special muscle systems to help us move.)

Some ancient cities used to have thick walls around them to protect them from foreign invaders. The body has a protective wall around it too, called the skin.

A very important part of the life of the city is the processing and distribution of food and other materials. Raw materials are brought in from the countryside, and in special factories in the city

5

they may be cooked or cut up or frozen, packaged, and sent to local stores where the people of the city can buy enough for their own needs. In the body there is a special system called the digestive system, which provides for the intake of raw materials, breaks them down into substances the cells can use, and then sends them in convenient-sized packages to the various parts of the body.

Some of the food is used by the body for building new parts and repairing old ones. But some is used as fuel and burned for energy. Oxygen is needed for this burning. In the city, oxygen is to be found in the air. But oxygen must be brought into the body by a special system called the respiratory system. When food is burned, waste products, especially carbon dioxide, are formed. Many of these waste products pass out of the body again through the respiratory system.

3
Our Respiratory System

Getting oxygen from the air to the cells of the body is not as simple as it might seem. Most of the trillions of cells of our bodies are locked away inside, shielded by layers and layers of other cells. Air enters the body through the passages that make up the respiratory system.

The gateways to the respiratory system are the nose and mouth. You can test this by trying an experiment which you have probably done many times before, but perhaps never really thought about. You know that you can breathe through your nose with your mouth closed. Now hold your nose tightly closed and breathe through your mouth. Air can easily go in and out this way too.

But you may notice a difference. When you breathe through your mouth, the air reaching your throat feels much cooler than when you breathe through your nose. Air is warmed as it passes through your nose. It is also moistened there. Air is not moistened as well when it passes through your mouth. That is why your throat may become dry when you have a cold and have to breathe through your mouth.

The nose also acts as a "guardian of the gates." If you touch the openings of your nostrils, you can feel bristly little hairs. These act as a sort of screen or trap: they catch bits of dust and other particles from the air and keep them from getting far into your nose. Particles too small to be trapped by the screen of hairs in your nostrils are stopped farther along the passages of your nose—they are caught in the sticky lining. The sticky substance that lines the passages of the respiratory system is called mucus. When you have a cold, your body makes much more mucus than usual, and that is what makes your nose "run."

The passages from the nose and mouth meet in a chamber called the pharynx (pronounced FAR-ingks). The pharynx leads into two new passage-

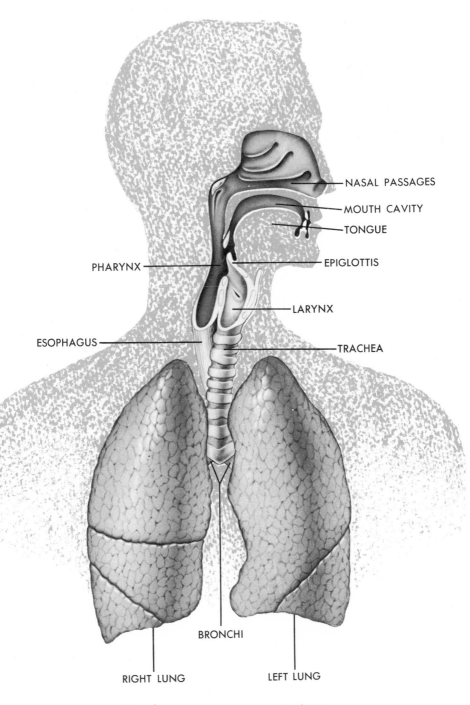

NASAL PASSAGES

MOUTH CAVITY

TONGUE

PHARYNX

EPIGLOTTIS

LARYNX

ESOPHAGUS

TRACHEA

BRONCHI

RIGHT LUNG

LEFT LUNG

The human respiratory system.

ways. One is open, and the other is guarded by a trap door called the epiglottis (ep-i-GLOT-tis). The open passageway, called the esophagus (e-SOF-a-gus), leads down into the stomach and is part of the digestive system. The guarded passageway, called the trachea (TRAY-kee-a), leads down to the lungs and is part of the respiratory system.

You may wonder why food and air, passing down the pharynx, do not often get mixed up and "go down the wrong pipe." The epiglottis neatly prevents such a mixup. When we swallow food or water, the trap door of the epiglottis clamps down tight and shuts off the trachea. Then the food and water pass down through the only open passageway: the esophagus. Once in a while the epiglottis does not close down fast enough when we swallow, and a bit of food or water does get into the trachea. Then we cough and sputter until it is out again.

At the top of the trachea, just under the epiglottis, there is a widened chamber. This is the voice box or larynx (LAR-ingks). Two tough bands of an elastic tissue are stretched out across the passageway of the voice box. When air passes by them it sets them vibrating, just as you can make a stretched rubber band vibrate by plucking on it. This vibration comes out of our mouths as sounds when we speak or sing. You can feel the vibrations of your own larynx if you place your fingertips on the front of your neck, just below the chin, and talk.

From the pharynx, air passes down the larynx and through the trachea. The walls of the trachea are made of firm but elastic rings of cartilage, a gristle-like tissue. You can actually feel them with your fingers if you press gently on the front of your neck.

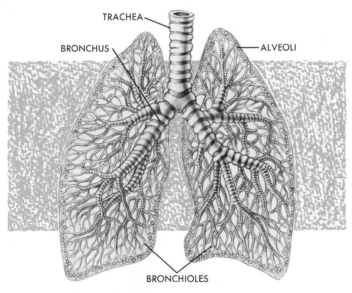

The human lungs.

11

Going downward, the trachea branches into two smaller passageways, whose walls are also made of elastic rings. These passageways are called the bronchi (BRONG-kye); one leads into the left lung, and the other into the right lung. Each bronchus branches again and again into smaller and smaller passageways, the tiniest of which are bronchioles (BRONG-kee-oles).

Each bronchiole ends in a little air-filled sac called an alveolus (al-VEE-oh-lus). These alveoli are grouped together in clusters, like bunches of grapes. There are millions and millions of them,

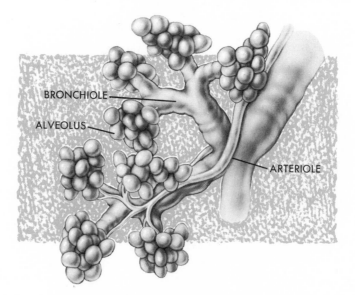

Closeup of air sacs in the human lung.

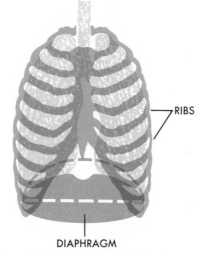

RIBS

DIAPHRAGM

The "cage" that contains the lungs.

and together they make up our lungs. It is through the walls of the alveoli that air passes from the lungs into the bloodstream, where it is then carried throughout the body.

Our lungs are quite remarkable. If we could take the walls of all the alveoli from a single pair of lungs and make clothing from them, we would have enough "material" to cover a hundred people from head to foot!

Both lungs fit snugly within the chest cavity of our bodies. The lungs are protected by a cage of bones called the ribs. Below the lungs is a thick dome-shaped muscle called the diaphragm (DIE-uh-fram). This muscle forms a floor for the bone

13

cage and can move up and down. It plays a very important part in our breathing. Other muscles are found between the ribs, and they too play an important part in the way we breathe.

4
How We Breathe

The air about us is made up of a mixture of gases. About four fifths of it is a gas called nitrogen. Though nitrogen is the most plentiful of all the gases in the air, in the gas form it is not very important to our bodies. But there is another gas in the air that is so important to us that we could not live for more than a few minutes without it. This is the gas called oxygen, which makes up about a fifth of the air that we breathe. There are also small amounts of other gases, such as carbon dioxide, as well as some water vapor.

As we have seen, when we inhale, air passes in through the nose, down the trachea, through the branching bronchi and bronchioles and into the alveoli, the tiny air sacs of the lungs. When we exhale, most of this air goes rushing out again. But why should the air enter in the first place? To understand this, we must learn a little physics.

The air around us is made up of tiny particles of gas, which scientists call molecules. A single molecule is much too small for us to see. But all the molecules are moving constantly, somewhat like bouncing Ping-Pong balls. They zip through the air, bouncing about as they bump into each other, and into the walls of the room, the furniture, and our bodies. Wherever they bounce, they strike with a certain force. The more molecules that strike a particular place, the greater the force. Scientists speak of the force on a certain area as pressure and say that the air "exerts a pressure" on the surface.

Usually we do not notice the pressure of the air molecules around us, just as we do not usually notice the touch of the clothes we are wearing. We are used to them. But if there is a change in pressure, we do notice it. For instance, place your hand in front of your mouth and blow on it. As

you blow, you are forcing extra billions and billions of air molecules against your hand. Now you are aware of the air pressure.

Inside our lungs the air molecules exert a pressure, just as they do in the air around us. We might think of our lungs as balloons, containing tiny bouncing molecules.

Imagine a large balloon, five feet in diameter, with walls of a strange new stretchable plastic, so clear that you can see through it. Inside are ten bouncing Ping-Pong balls. These are not ordinary Ping-Pong balls, for they keep on moving and never stop. As they move, they strike the walls of the balloon and bounce off in all directions.

If we looked at one small part of the wall of the balloon (for instance, a place the size of a silver dollar) and counted the number of times a Ping-Pong ball hit that spot each minute, we might find that there were, let us say, about ten hits each minute.

Now imagine blowing the balloon up so that it is a giant balloon, 25 feet in diameter. There is more than a hundred times more space in the balloon. But there are still only ten Ping-Pong balls inside it. Each now has much farther to travel before it hits a wall, and there is much more wall space for it to hit. If we looked at a spot the size of a silver dollar, we might have to wait more than a minute before it was hit even once. And since the spot we are looking at is hit much less often, the force that the balls exert on that spot is smaller, and so the pressure is lower. This is also true of any other spot on the balloon. Thus, when the balloon gets larger, the pressure inside it drops.

Now let most of the air out of the balloon, so that it shrinks to only one foot in diameter. You would let the air out carefully, so that no Ping-Pong balls would escape. Now the ten Ping-Pong balls are squeezed into a much smaller space. And as they keep moving, they bounce more often off the walls. A spot the size of a silver dollar might be hit more than a thousand times in a single minute. And so, when the balloon gets smaller, the pressure inside it goes up.

Suppose now that there are two jars of the same size, connected at the mouths. One jar contains 25 bouncing Ping-Pong balls, while the other one contains only five. The pressure of the Ping-Pong balls inside the jar with 25 is much greater than in the one with only five. But as the balls bounce around, they go flying in all directions. Some escape from one jar into the other. Since one jar has many more balls to start with, probably more balls will reach its mouth and bounce into the other jar. After a while there will be about 15 Ping-Pong balls in

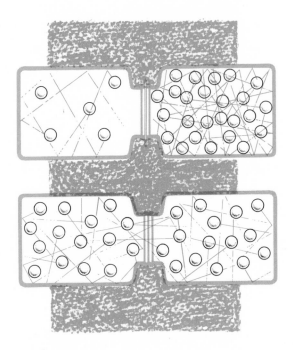

The "pressures" of bouncing Ping Pong balls are gradually equalized.

each jar. The pressures will be just about equal. In a similar way, air usually moves from places of higher pressure to places of lower pressure.

Pressures play an important part in the way we breathe. When we breathe in, the diaphragm—the tough muscle that forms the floor of the chest cavity—moves downward. (Scientists say that the diaphragm "contracts.") At the same time, the muscles between the ribs also contract. They pull upon the ribs and bring them up and outward. With the floor moving down and the walls moving outward, the whole chest cavity grows larger. The balloon-like lungs swell too. This causes the air pressure inside the lungs to drop.

But the pressure of the air in the room outside our bodies has not changed. Now it is greater than the pressure inside our expanded lungs. And the room and our lungs are connected through the trachea and bronchi. So air comes rushing into our lungs, until the pressure in them is again equal to the pressure in the outside room.

When we breathe out, the opposite occurs—it is almost like watching a movie run backward. The diaphragm relaxes until it is an upward-curving dome again. The rib muscles relax, and the ribs move down. And so, with the floor moving up and the walls moving down, the chest cavity becomes smaller. Now the lungs are pressed inward, and there is not as much space for the air molecules to move around. The pressure inside the lungs rises. Now it is greater than the pressure in the room. The air is forced out until the pressures are again equal.

You may wonder what makes the rib muscles and the diaphragm contract in the first place. We

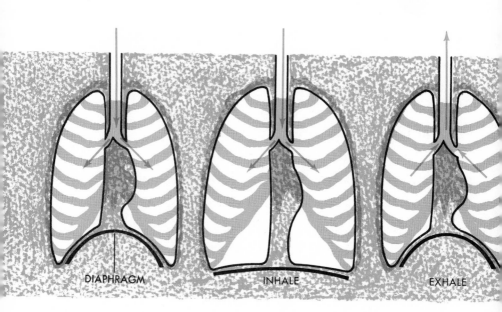

DIAPHRAGM   INHALE   EXHALE

As we breathe in, the rib muscles pull the ribs out and up, and the diaphragm moves downward; as we breathe out, the rib muscles relax, the ribs move downward, and the diaphragm moves up.

never have to think about contracting these muscles. We can watch television or read a book or eat dinner or even go to sleep, and the muscles keep working and we go on breathing in and out.

A special part of the brain acts as a central signal station. It sends signals to the diaphragm and rib muscles to tell them when to contract. This part of the brain is called the breathing center.

22

You may wonder how the breathing center knows when to send the signals. A special chemical called carbon dioxide acts as a trigger. When there is a certain amount of it in the blood reaching the brain, it "tells" the breathing center that it is time to send out another signal.

Just how does the carbon dioxide get into the blood? The answer lies in another important part of the story of breathing—the exchange of gases in our bodies.

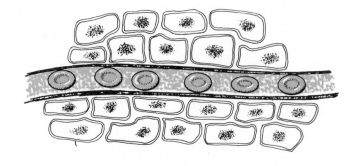

5
The Gas Exchange

What happens to air when it reaches the lungs? If we just breathed in air and then breathed the same air out again, there would seem to be no benefit to breathing. But this is not what happens. The air that we breathe out has more carbon dioxide and less oxygen than the air we breathe in. We already know that the body uses oxygen to help it produce energy. Let us see exactly what happens to oxygen when it enters our body.

The tiny air sacs of the lungs, or alveoli, have very thin walls. These walls are so thin that gas molecules can pass right through. Each alveolus is like a basket made of chicken wire, in which Ping-Pong balls are bouncing. Some balls bounce on the wires, but others go right through the holes.

Clinging to the outside of the wall of each alveolus is a tiny blood vessel called a capillary. Each capillary is so small that you cannot see it without a microscope. And its walls are just as thin as the walls of the alveoli.

When new air comes into the lungs, oxygen molecules pass out through the walls of the alveoli and into the capillaries surrounding them, because there is much more oxygen in the alveoli than in the blood in the surrounding capillaries. And just as in the case of the bouncing Ping-Pong balls which gradually moved from one jar to the other, gas molecules tend to move from a place where there are more molecules to a place where there are fewer.

There is also some carbon dioxide in the air that we breathe in, but there is much more carbon dioxide in the blood flowing in the capillaries around the alveoli. (We will explain why this is so later on.) And so carbon dioxide molecules tend to pass *into* the alveoli from the capillaries.

Floating along in the blood flowing through the capillaries are millions of red blood cells. Each one looks like a little doughnut without the hole in the middle. Each red blood cell contains a red chemical called hemoglobin. This chemical has a

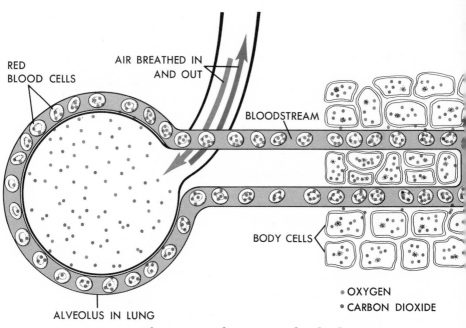

RED
BLOOD CELLS

AIR BREATHED IN
AND OUT

BLOODSTREAM

BODY CELLS

• OXYGEN
• CARBON DIOXIDE

ALVEOLUS IN LUNG

The gas exchange in the body.

very special ability. It can join with either oxygen or carbon dioxide.

The red blood cells reaching the lungs are like little ferryboats. They carry a load of carbon dioxide that they have picked up in various parts of the body. At the alveoli, the hemoglobin of the red blood cells unloads its carbon dioxide and picks up a new cargo of oxygen. The carbon dioxide passes into the alveoli, up through the bronchioles and bronchi, past the trachea, through the nose, and out of the body in the air that we breathe

26

out. The oxygen begins a journey through the body along the bloodstream.

Each of the cells of the body needs a constant supply of oxygen, for the living cell is the center of furious activity. In nearly every cell more than a thousand different jobs are being done, and most of these jobs could not be done without a supply of energy.

The body's supplies of ready energy are stored in handy chemical packets called ATP. ATP is made by the cell itself. The process by which it is made is very complicated. It includes many different steps, in which chemicals are changed from one form to another. The making of ATP is called cellular respiration; it is a process that needs oxygen.

In a way, cellular respiration is very much like burning. When you light a campfire, you need fuel to burn. But you also need air to keep it going. If you covered the fire with a large glass dome so that no new air could get to it, the fire would quickly go out.

In cellular respiration, the cell "burns" some of its chemicals, mainly sugars, to gain the energy locked inside them. But the "burning" inside the cell is very different from the kind of burning that occurs when you light a campfire. As the sticks and dry leaves of the campfire burn, the energy stored inside them is wasted as heat and light. But the cell does not waste much of its energy. In the "burning" of cellular respiration there are no bright flames. Instead, the "burning" takes place in a number of small steps. And with each step, the energy released is carefully stored away in a little packet of ATP. (Some heat is given off and helps to keep the body warm.)

There is another difference between the burning of a campfire and the "burning" that takes place inside the cell. Most of the sticks and dry leaves of the campfire are not burned completely. When the fire has burned itself out, there is a pile of black charcoal—the chemical called carbon—left. In cellular respiration, most of the carbon is combined with oxygen and changed to carbon dioxide.

But carbon dioxide is a dangerous waste product for the cell. Too much can poison it. The red cell ferryboats that have unloaded their cargo of oxygen pick up a new cargo of carbon dioxide and carry it back along the bloodstream to the lungs.

It is the carbon dioxide in the blood that acts as a signal and stimulates the breathing center in the brain to send messages to the diaphragm and rib muscles.

The exchange of gases that takes place when we breathe also takes place in most other living creatures. Dogs and cows, mice, whales, and even snakes have lungs and breathe very much the way we do. But many other animals, such as fish and insects, do not have lungs. Plants do not have lungs either. Yet they all need oxygen and must get rid of their waste carbon dioxide. Each has its own way of breathing and its own special breathing organs.

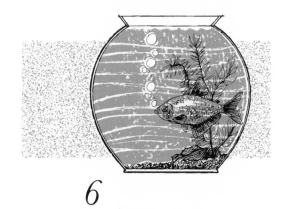

6
How Fish Breathe

Fish spend all their lives underwater. But you and I could stay underwater safely for only a few minutes, unless we carried our air with us in special tanks.

Some of the air from the atmosphere that we breathe dissolves into the water of seas and ponds, rivers and lakes. Fish and most other water animals get all the air they need from the water itself.

How can they breathe water without drowning? Fish, clams, octopuses, crabs, and other water animals do not have lungs as we do. Instead, they have special underwater breathing devices called gills, with which they filter out the oxygen they need from the water in which they live.

If you look at a fish, you will notice several slits on each side of its body, a small distance to the rear of its eyes. These are the gill slits. If you bend the fish's body so that you can see inside these slitlike openings, you will find many rows of pink plates and branches of thin membranes, with many tiny blood vessels carrying rich red blood.

The thin membranes in the gills of a fish are very much like the thin walls of the alveoli in our lungs. And the same sort of exchange of gases, carbon dioxide and oxygen, takes place there.

A fish breathes by opening and closing its mouth regularly. When it opens its mouth, it draws in some water. Then it closes its mouth and squeezes its throat muscles, so that there is very little room inside its mouth. The water has nowhere to go but backward, out through the gills, and then out of the fish's body through the gill slits.

Before the water flows out through the gill slits, it passes over the many plates and branches of the gills. Oxygen molecules pass through the thin membranes into the tiny blood vessels, and from there are carried through the fish's body to supply all its cells. Meanwhile, just as in our lungs, carbon dioxide that had been carried from the body

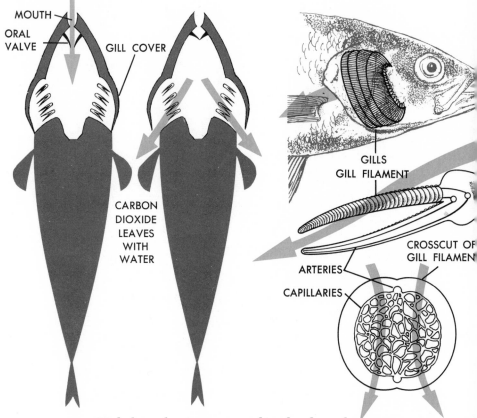

Fish breathe in oxygen dissolved in the water.

cells to the gills passes out of the blood vessels, through the membrane, and into the current of water flowing out. This exchange of gases takes place for the same reason that it does in the human body. Since there is less oxygen in the blood vessels than in the water, the oxygen molecules pass

32

through the membranes and into the blood vessels. But since there is more carbon dioxide in the fish's bloodstream than in the water, the carbon dioxide travels the other way through the membranes, out into the water.

Since there is oxygen in sea water (although much less than in the air that we breathe), scientists have long wondered whether there might be some way that man could use this oxygen. If this were possible, we would be able to explore the oceans and might even be able to live under the sea.

Recently scientists have devised an artificial gill, made of plastic membranes. A person breathes in and out through a face mask, which is attached to the artificial gills by hoses. He gets oxygen from the air dissolved in the water. And, just as in a fish's gills, his waste carbon dioxide passes out through the membrane into the water. The artificial gills that we have now are much too big and bulky for a diver to carry around with him. But it is hoped that new ones can be made which will be much smaller and more convenient to carry.

Some even more exciting studies of underwater breathing have been made. Since the exchange of gases in our lungs is very much like that in a fish's gills, scientists have actually pumped water into the lungs of land animals, such as mice and dogs. This was very special water, in which much more oxygen than usual was dissolved. And fresh, oxygen-filled water had to be pumped in regularly, so that the lungs would receive a supply of fresh oxygen. But the animals were actually able to breathe water, and after the experiment was over, they were as healthy as before.

Perhaps experiments such as these will someday lead to man's building cities under the sea and swimming about underwater as freely as a fish.

7

How Insects Breathe

Every now and then a science fiction horror movie is made in which giant insects, a hundred feet tall, threaten the people of the earth. Fortunately for us, such nightmare creatures could never exist. Insects simply could not survive if they grew that large. Even insects a few feet tall could not live in our world.

One of the main reasons why insects cannot grow very large has to do with the way they breathe. An insect is built something like a Swiss cheese. Its respiratory system is made up of countless numbers of holes and channels running through its body. If a Swiss cheese got too large, it would collapse, because there would be too

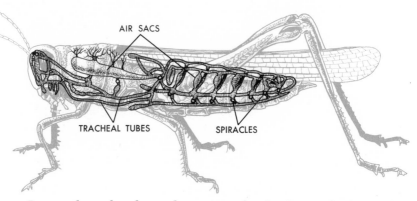

AIR SACS

TRACHEAL TUBES

SPIRACLES

Insects breathe through a network of tubes, which open out to the air.

much empty space inside for the cheese to support. In the same way, a giant insect could not support itself and would quickly be crushed by its own weight.

An insect's respiratory system is actually much simpler than ours. Air passes in through many holes along the sides of its body. These holes are called spiracles (SPEAR-uh-kls). The holes, which the insect can open and close with special circular muscles, lead inside the body along air pipes called tracheal tubes. The tracheal tubes branch and branch again. Tiny branches lead to all parts of the insect's body.

No bloodstream carries gases through the insect's body. Air travels along the tracheal tubes, and oxygen passes through the walls of the tubes directly to each cell of the body. The waste carbon dioxide passes out through the walls, along the tubes, and out of the body through the spiracles. And again, this occurs because there is less oxygen in the cells than in the air in the tracheal tubes, and more carbon dioxide.

When insects are actively moving about, their spiracles open and close much more often than when they are at rest. And in many insects contractions of the body muscles help to pump air in and out something like a bellows.

Just as in our bodies, the rate at which insects breathe is controlled by messages sent along the nerves by special breathing centers. And these breathing centers are told when to send their signals by the amount of carbon dioxide that reaches them.

Insects that live in the water have special breathing problems. Since they do not have gills, they cannot breathe the oxygen dissolved in the water. Some insects cannot stay underwater for very long. Just like human swimmers, they must come up for air quite often. But other insects can take air supplies underwater with them, as human

deep-sea divers do. A little beetle called the whirl-igig carries a bubble of air clasped between the tips of its wings. When it swims underwater it uses this air to breathe. The water boatman, another beetle, carries a thin film of air over its body, covering it like a sparkling suit of clothes. This air is as buoyant as a life preserver, and makes the water boatman bob up and down in the water as it swims.

Spiders do not belong to the insect family, even though many people think of them as "bugs." But spiders do have spiracles and tracheal tubes to help them breathe.

These strange animals have another kind of respiratory system in addition—structures called "book lungs." These book lungs are found in the spider's abdomen, and they are built very much like gills. They are made of layers of membranes that are folded like the pages of a book. However, they are used for breathing air, not water. Spiders that live in the water must bring an air supply along with them when they dive, just as the water insects do.

One kind of water spider spins a bell-shaped web underwater and fastens it carefully to water plants with her strong silk. Then she climbs up to the surface along a thread that she has left attached to a floating leaf. When she scampers down again to her silken bell, she carries with her tiny sparkling bubbles of air, clinging to her hairy legs and body. Leaving the air bubbles trapped under her web, she climbs up to the surface for more. Up and down she goes, again and again, until her airtight web is bulging upward, like a balloon filled with gas. Now the water spider has a dry, air-filled home in which to live.

8
Odd Ways of Breathing

There are invisible worlds all about us, inhabited by swarms of creatures so small that we cannot see them without a microscope. These living organisms are to be found in ponds and streams, in the soil that we walk upon, and even in the air that we breathe. The puddles that form by the side of the road when it rains quickly become filled with such tiny creatures. Most of these microorganisms, as they are called, consist of just a single cell.

None of the cells in our bodies could live all alone. They depend on other cells to feed them or protect them. But single-celled microorganisms can do all the things needed to live. They can grow and reproduce. They eat or make their own food.

Many of them can move about. Some ooze along the muddy bottom of ponds and streams. Others are propelled through the water by long lashing "tails" called flagella, or by rows of tiny hairlike structures called cilia, which beat back and forth like oars.

Like us, these one-celled microorganisms need energy for all their activities. And nearly all of them need oxygen to burn their food to provide this energy.

Yet how can they take in oxygen? A one-celled creature does not have lungs or gills or spiracles. These structures are made up of thousands, millions, or—as in our own lungs—many billions of cells.

Most of the one-celled microorganisms breathe in a very simple way. The outer surface of the cell is a thin membrane, something like a sieve or strainer. Small molecules, such as oxygen and carbon dioxide, can pass readily in and out. As the animal swims through the water, oxygen from the water passes inside, and carbon dioxide passes out. These flows of gases occur because as these cells "burn" their food, oxygen is used up and carbon dioxide is produced.

Many more complicated water-dwelling animals also breathe through the outer surface of their bodies. In ponds and streams, tiny ribbon-like flatworms can be found, barely longer than the tip of a finger. They creep along the bottom and hide under rocks and plant leaves. These flatworms are made up of millions of cells. They have eyes and even a little brain. But much like their one-celled neighbors in the pond, they have no respiratory organs. Oxygen passes in through the outer surface of the worm's body, and carbon dioxide passes out.

In the same pond, frogs might be found, swimming through the water or basking in the sunlight on the bank. Frogs are much more complicated than flatworms. Their bodies are made of billions and billions of cells. They can see and hear. They have special organs for digesting their food and getting rid of their waste products. They even have lungs, just as we do.

But frogs also breathe through their skins. A frog must keep its skin moist at all times, because oxygen from the air dissolves into a moist film around the frog's body. From this film, it passes through the skin into countless numbers of capil-

Gradually the tadpole changes from a gill-breathing water creature to a lung-breathing frog, which can go out on land.

laries just beneath the surface. If a frog stayed in the sun too long and its skin dried out, it would soon die, for its lungs are not efficient enough to meet all its needs for oxygen. That is why frogs always stay close to the water and dive in every now and then.

In the late fall, when the weather is getting cold and the ponds will soon be freezing over, frogs bury themselves in the mud at the bottom. There they hibernate, or sleep the winter through. During this long sleep they "breathe" only through their skins, for their lungs cannot work under water.

Frogs are not born with lungs. Frogs' eggs hatch into tiny fishlike tadpoles which breathe through gills just like fish. For the next few months these tadpoles daily grow larger and larger. Soon a strange series of changes begins. Legs appear where there were none before—first the hind legs, then the forelegs. One of the strangest of these changes is the development of two tiny buds which grow, day by day, into a pair of lungs. The tadpole's gills disappear. Now it is a frog. No longer does it have to stay in the water all the time. It can leap out of the water and hop about on the banks, breathing air with its new lungs.

9
How Plants Breathe

A grassy meadow seems peaceful from a distance. But look close and it is bustling with activity. Rabbits hop about, nibbling on the grass. Field mice scurry along, busily looking for food and taking cover when danger threatens. Bright-colored butterflies flit about from flower to flower. And smaller insects hum and buzz and dart about.

All these animals seem so alive! But what of the grass and the trees? They are alive too. They do not seem to move, except when the wind sways them. And yet they are moving, very slowly, as they grow. Their leaves turn to follow the sun as it moves across the sky, and their roots grow down into the earth, stretching out toward sources of water.

Like animals, plants such as grass and trees need energy for their many activities. And they need oxygen to burn fuel to supply this energy.

Plants do not have lungs or gills to breathe with. And the top parts of plants cannot "breathe through their moist skin" as frogs and flatworms do, for the outer surface of most plant cells is covered with a wax-coated wall. This wall keeps out water and gases. You can see this if you place a drop of water on a plant leaf. The water remains in the form of a round drop. It does not spread out. But if you place a drop of water on a piece of newspaper or cardboard (make sure the cardboard does not have a shiny waxy coating), the drop spreads out into a thin film and quickly soaks through.

But air does get into the plant through the leaves. How does this happen? On the underside of the leaf (and in many plants on the stems as well), there are thousands and thousands of tiny openings. These openings are called stomata (pronounced sto-MA-ta). Each opening or stoma (STO-ma) is guarded by a pair of bean-shaped cells. As you might expect, they are called guard cells. Their job is to open and close the stomata— the gateways to the leaf—according to the amount

47

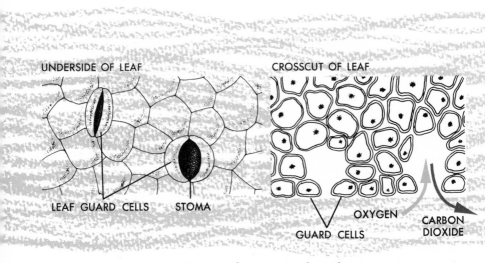

UNDERSIDE OF LEAF

CROSSCUT OF LEAF

LEAF GUARD CELLS   STOMA

OXYGEN

CARBON DIOXIDE

GUARD CELLS

Gas exchange in the plant.

of sunlight and the humidity of the air. When the stomata are open, gases can pass in and out easily.

The roots of plants, which are in the soil, need air too. They get their oxygen by a process similar to the way in which flatworms and frogs breathe. Millions of tiny root hairs spread out into the soil from the tips of the roots. These root hairs are covered with a film of moisture, just as the frog's skin is. There is much air in the soil, caught in numerous small pockets. Air from these pockets dissolves in the film of moisture on the root hairs. There is no waxy covering on the root hairs, and so gas molecules can pass easily in and out.

If plants were not able to breathe through their roots, they would soon die. They would suffocate, just as we would if we had no air. For the roots cannot get enough oxygen from the flow of materials from the leaves. That is one reason why farmers dig and turn over the soil around their plants, to loosen it. In this way they make more pockets in which air can be trapped. Worms and other burrowing animals also help to loosen the soil and thus help plants to live and grow.

10

Gas Cycles on the Earth

What would happen if all the plants on the earth suddenly died?

First of all, all the animals that eat only plants would die. Cows and horses would die. Rabbits and field mice would die. So would tadpoles and minnows.

Soon the seas would be filled with starving fish. And the lands would be covered with starving foxes and owls and other hunters, for these hunters prey upon animals that eat plants.

Finally man too, with first his crops and then his food animals gone, would be faced with starvation. But let us suppose that man discovered a way to make food for himself artificially and cheaply.

With his factories turning out food, would he now be saved?

No! For the death of all the plants would eventually bring even deeper changes to our world.

As the people of the earth continued to breathe and to burn fuel both in their own bodies and in factories, cars, and homes, they would be taking in oxygen and giving off carbon dioxide. Gradually the oxygen in the air would grow scarcer. And there would be more and more carbon dioxide in the air.

Carbon dioxide is a very heavy gas, and it would stay close to the ground. Thus it would form a blanket over the earth.

In today's world, sunlight strikes the earth and warms it. Much of this warmth is given off into outer space. But if the earth were covered with a heavy blanket of carbon dioxide, most of the warmth would be kept near the surface. As a result, the average temperature of the earth would rise and rise. In time, it would rise above 100 degrees and still further, perhaps eventually reaching hundreds of degrees.

Even if man stayed in air-conditioned buildings, after a while there would be so much carbon di-

The green plants of the world help to keep the gases of the atmosphere in balance.

oxide in the air that it would be poisonous to breathe.

We said that all of this could happen if all the plants on the earth suddenly died. For plants play many important roles in nature. In addition to serving as food for animals, they also help to keep in balance the amounts of carbon dioxide and oxygen in our atmosphere.

The green plants of our world use not only oxygen from the air, but also much larger amounts of

Man and his machinery add carbon dioxide to the atmosphere.

carbon dioxide. In sunlight they combine this carbon dioxide with water and turn these simple chemicals into sugars and other complicated chemicals of life. This process is called photosynthesis. And one of its by-products is oxygen.

Photosynthesis is the opposite of respiration. In respiration complicated chemicals are combined with oxygen and broken down into water and carbon dioxide. In the process, their stored energy is released. In photosynthesis, water and carbon

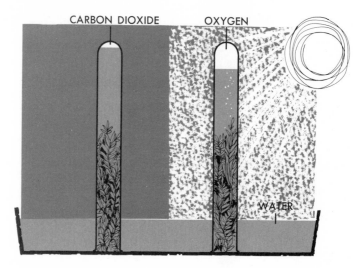

An experiment to show that plants produce carbon dioxide by respiration and oxygen through photosynthesis.

dioxide are combined into complicated chemicals. In the process, energy is stored and oxygen is released.

Plants go on "breathing" night and day. But they can photosynthesize only during the day, when the sunlight strikes them. During the night they take in oxygen and "breathe out" carbon dioxide, just as we do. But in the daytime, much more carbon dioxide is used up in photosynthesis than is formed during respiration. And so in the daytime, plants give off a great deal of oxygen.

They give off so much more oxygen than they take in, that they help to replace the oxygen that the animals of the earth use up.

You can test this with a simple experiment. All you will need are two test tubes or long, narrow pill bottles, two cups or shallow cans, and some green water plants. (You can get these plants from a pond or from a pet shop that sells fish.) Stuff each test tube half-full with green plants. Then fill both test tubes completely with water. Place a small piece of cardboard over the top of one of the test tubes, and holding it tightly, turn the test tube upside down and place it in a cup half-filled with water. Then remove the cardboard. Be careful not to let any air bubbles get inside the test tube. Now turn the other test tube over in the same way.

Place one tube in bright sunlight and the other in a dark closet. After a while, you can see thousands of tiny bubbles forming on the leaves of the water plants in the sun. The bubbles rise to the top of the tube. Soon there is a pocket of gas, which gradually grows larger and larger.

After several hours, slip a small piece of cardboard under the mouth of the sunlit test tube. Now carefully turn it over again. Keep the cardboard tightly over the top. Have a friend set a thin piece of wood aflame with a match. Now have him blow out the flame of the wood splint so that it is just glowing a dull red. Quickly take the cover off the test tube and plunge the glowing splint into the gas (which is on the top now). Suddenly the splint will burst into flame again—brighter than before. This shows that the gas in the tube was oxygen.

Now look at the test tube from the dark closet. Probably there will be very little gas at the top of the tube. If you test this gas in the same way (provided you have enough gas to test), you will find that the glow of the splint actually goes out completely. This gas is not oxygen; it is carbon dioxide. Since the plant was out of the sunlight, it carried on only respiration, and not photosynthesis.

We can see that animals and plants are dependent upon one another through the cycles of gases: carbon dioxide and oxygen. Plants cannot make their food without the carbon dioxide that animals give out. (The plants' own respiration alone would not supply enough.) Animals could not breathe and gain energy through respiration without the oxygen that photosynthesizing plants give off.

Respiration is a vital process for living things, from invisible microorganisms to the giants of the plant and animal world.

Index

energy, 2, 6, 27, 28, 42, 47, 53

epiglottis, 10

esophagus, 10

excretory system, 5

fish, 30–34

flatworms, 43

frogs, 43–44

gas cycles, 50–56

gas exchange, 24–29, 31–33, 37, 42, 43, 48

gills, 30–34, 45

gills, artificial, 33

guard cells, 47

hemoglobin, 25, 26

insects, 35–38

larynx, 10, 11

lungs, 13, 16, 21, 29, 34, 44, 45

microorganisms, 41, 42

molecules, 16

mouth, 7, 8

mucus, 8

nervous system, 5

nitrogen, 15

nose, 7, 8, 15, 26

oxygen, 2, 6, 7, 15, 24–29, 31–33, 37, 43, 48, 51–56

pharynx, 8, 11

photosynthesis, 53–56

plants, 46–49, 50–57

pressure, 16, 17, 19–21

red blood cells, 25, 26, 28

respiration, 2

respiratory system, 2, 6, 7

respiratory system of
  fish, 30, 31
  frogs, 43–45
  insects, 35–37
  man, 7–14
  spiders, 38, 39

ribs, 13, 14, 20–22

root hairs, 48

skin, 5, 43–44

spiders, 38–40

spiracles, 36–38